Parents' notes

This book has been designed to help young children learn their first French words and phrases. It is best to use the book together so you can assist with pronunciation. At the back of the book is an easy pronunciation guide which you can use as a guideline.
Each double page spread clearly illustrates words relating to everyday life at home, in the shops and around a town, labelling them both in French and English. By looking at the pictures together and using the French names for things, your child will soon begin to develop a vocabulary of common French words.

© 1980 Usborne Publishing Ltd.
© 1991 Usborne Publishing Ltd. for the French text.
Usborne House,
83-85 Saffron Hill,
London EC1N 8RT,
England.

Printed in Belgium

The name Usborne and the device are Trade Marks of Usborne Publishing Ltd.

All rights reserved. No part of this publication may be reproduced, stored in a retrieval system or transmitted in any form or by any means, electronic, mechanical, photocopying, recording or otherwise, without the prior permission of the publisher.

Read French

Carol Watson
Illustrated by Colin King

Translation: Marie-Lorraine Sharp

Series Editor: Heather Amery

Consultant: Betty Root

The House
La Maison

It has
Elle a

a very tall chimney,
une très haute cheminée,

a bright red roof,
un toit rouge vif,

five windows
cinq fenêtres

and a big green door.
et une grande porte verte.

The dog chases the cat
Le chien poursuit le chat

across the sink,
sur l'évier,

under the cooker,
sous la cuisinière,

over the table
par-dessus la table

and round the bin.
et autour de la poubelle.

They knock down
Ils font tomber

cups and saucers,
des tasses et des soucoupes,

a big saucepan,
une grande casserole,

a plate of cakes
une assiette de gâteaux

and the red apron.
et le tablier rouge.

The decorators have come to paint the living room.
Les peintres sont venus peindre la salle de séjour.

We take down
On enlève

the three pictures,
les trois tableaux,

the orange curtains,
les rideaux orange,

the old mirror
le vieux miroir

and the dusty clock.
et la pendule poussiéreuse.

They carry out
Ils sortent

the small table,
la petite table,

a big armchair,
un gros fauteuil,

the television
la télévision

and the rug.
et le tapis.

The decorators have finished.
Les peintres ont fini.

We help him to
Nous l'aidons à

wash the bonnet,
laver le capot,

polish the lights,
astiquer les phares,

clean the windscreen and the wheels.
nettoyer le pare-brise et les roues.

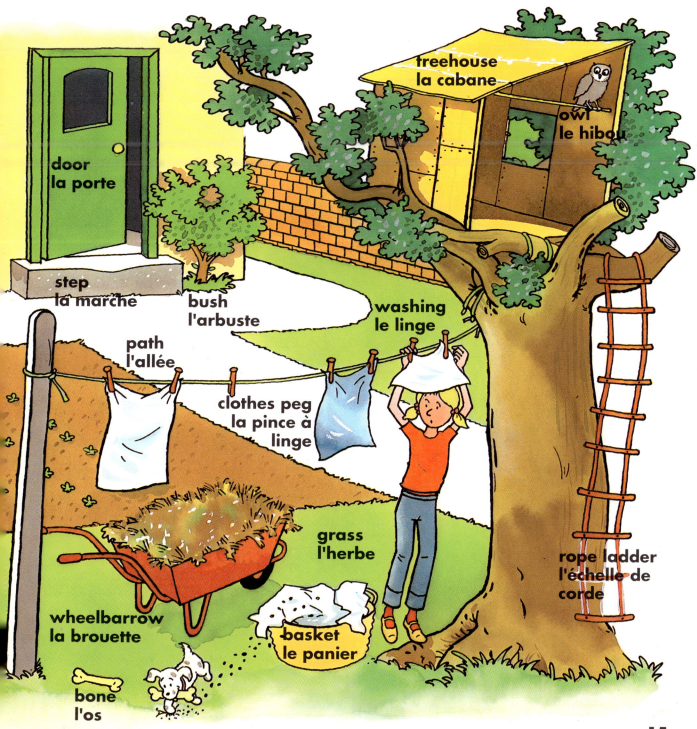

In the garden Dad likes to
Dans le jardin papa aime

dig the ground,
bêcher la terre,

plant seeds,
semer des graines,

water the flowers
arroser les fleurs

and sweep up the leaves.
et ramasser les feuilles.

We play in the garden.
Nous jouons dans le jardin.

We chase butterflies,
Nous courons après les papillons,

pick up worms,
ramassons des vers de terre,

hide in the bushes
nous cachons dans les buissons

and climb the trees.
et grimpons aux arbres.

In the bath
Dans le bain

we turn on the taps,
on ouvre les robinets,

we splash the water,
on éclabousse,

we make some bubbles
on fait des bulles

and we play with the soap.
et on joue avec le savon.

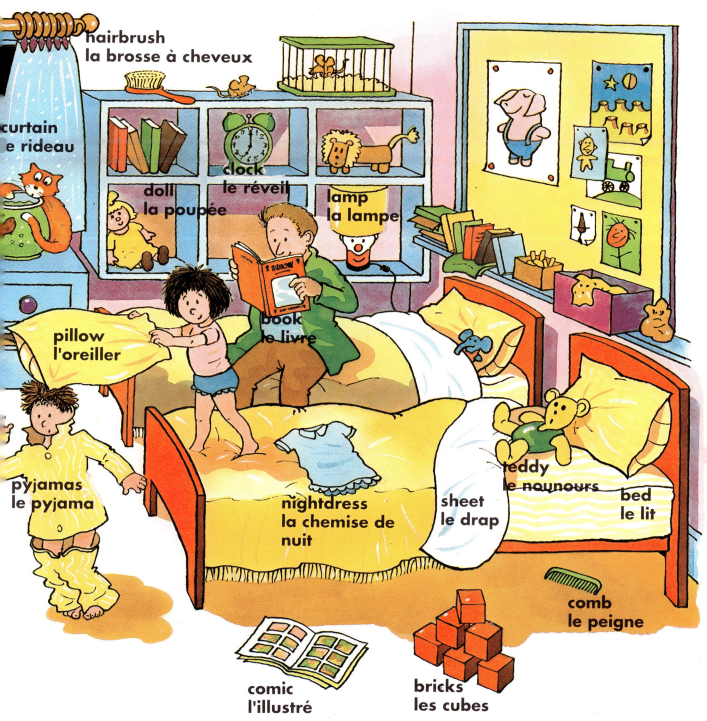

Off to bed!
Au lit!

We take off our shoes
Nous enlevons nos chaussures

and socks.
et nos chaussettes.

Where is the hairbrush?
Où est la brosse à cheveux?

Here is the comb!
Voici le peigne!

Dad puts us to bed.
Papa nous met au lit.

He reads a book to us,
Il nous lit un livre,

draws the curtains and kisses us goodnight.
tire les rideaux et nous embrasse en nous souhaitant bonne nuit.

Here is a puzzle.
Voici une devinette.

Can you find mum, dad, baby, the cat, two worms and the spotty dog?
Peux-tu trouver maman, papa, bébé, le chat, deux vers de terre et le chien tacheté?

The Shop
Le Magasin

The family goes shopping
La famille fait les courses

25

We are going shopping.
Nous allons faire les courses.

The shop has
Le magasin a

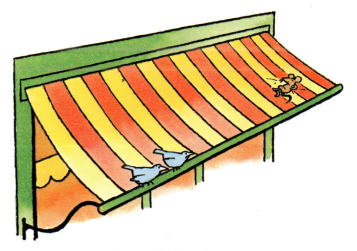

two big windows,
deux grandes vitrines,

a striped blind,
un store à rayures,

a newspaper stand
un tourniquet de journaux

and a shopkeeper.
et un marchand.

Mum wants
Maman a besoin

a basket
d'un panier

and a big trolley.
et d'un grand chariot.

We look at the bottles
Nous regardons les bouteilles

and tins.
et les conserves.

We take
Nous prenons

a box off the shelf,
une boîte sur l'étagère,

peas from the freezer,
des petits pois dans le congélateur,

apples from the barrel
des pommes dans le tonneau

and a packet of sugar.
et un paquet de sucre.

We look at the meat and fish.
Nous regardons la viande et le poisson.

We buy
Nous achetons

five chops,
cinq côtelettes,

two big fish,
deux gros poissons,

some sausages
des saucisses

and a fat chicken.
et un gros poulet.

Mum buys vegetables and fruit.
Maman achète des légumes et des fruits.

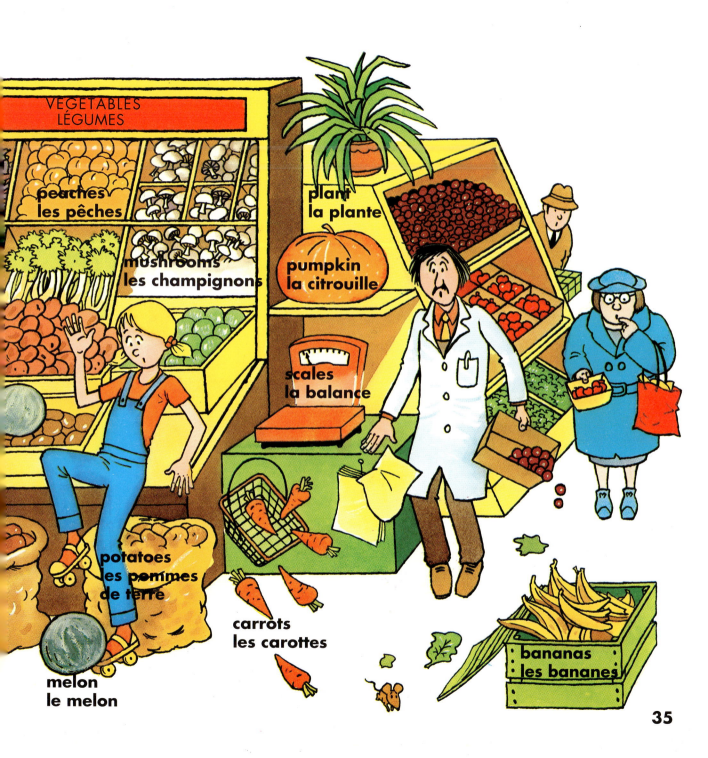

We pick up
Nous prenons

a few bananas,
quelques bananes,

a box of mushrooms,
une caisse de champignons,

a string of onions
un chapelet d'oignons

and two lettuces.
et deux laitues.

The man weighs
L'homme pèse

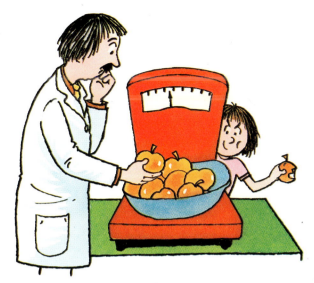

some apples
des pommes

and lots of carrots.
et beaucoup de carottes.

He drops a cabbage
Il laisse tomber un chou

and steps on a tomato.
et marche sur une tomate.

We find the bread and cakes.
Nous trouvons le pain et les gâteaux.

We take ten buns,
Nous prenons dix brioches,

some bread,
du pain,

a packet of biscuits
un paquet de biscuits

and a chocolate cake.
et un gâteau au chocolat.

We stop at the dairy counter.
Nous nous arrêtons au rayon crémerie.

We buy
Nous achetons

six pots of yoghurt,
six pots de yaourt,

two boxes of eggs,
deux boîtes d'oeufs,

three cartons of milk
trois cartons de lait

and some cheese.
et du fromage.

We find lots of things to read.
Nous trouvons beaucoup de choses à lire.

Mum stops to talk to her friends.
Maman s'arrête et bavarde avec ses amies.

We buy
On achète

some new pencils,
des crayons neufs,

coloured felt-tip pens
des feutres de couleur

and some sweets and chocolate for Dad.
et des bonbons et du chocolat pour papa.

At last we have finished.
Enfin nous avons fini.

Mum opens her purse and drops all her money.
Maman ouvre son porte-monnaie et laisse tomber tout son argent.

We pay the cashier,
Nous payons la caissière,

fill up the bags and off we go.
remplissons les sacs et en route.

Here is a puzzle.
Mum put these things into her bag.
Voici une devinette.
Maman a mis les choses suivantes dans son sac.

cake
le gâteau

carrots
les carottes

bananas
les bananes

chicken
le poulet

fish
le poisson

cheese
le fromage

eggs
les oeufs

sausages
les saucisses

lettuce
la laitue

Can you see what she lost on the way?
Vois-tu ce qu'elle a perdu en chemin?

Here is another puzzle.
Voici une autre devinette.

Can you find a bottle, a jar, a cake, some bread and a string of onions?
Peux-tu trouver une bouteille, un bocal, un gâteau, du pain et un chapelet d'oignons?

The Town
La Ville

The family goes to town
La famille va en ville

In the town there is
En ville il y a

a big hotel,
un grand hôtel,

a block of flats,
un immeuble,

a biscuit factory
une biscuiterie

and lots of shops.
et beaucoup de magasins.

Grandad is riding his bicycle. He goes past
Grand-père fait de la bicyclette. Il dépasse

a red van,
une camionnette rouge,

a big lorry,
un gros camion,

a yellow taxi
un taxi jaune

and the school bus.
et l'autobus de l'école.

We stop at the garage.
Nous nous arrêtons au garage.

We help the attendant
Nous aidons le garagiste

to put petrol in the tank,
à mettre de l'essence dans le réservoir,

oil in the engine,
de l'huile dans le moteur,

water in the radiator
de l'eau dans le radiateur

and to inflate the tyres.
et à gonfler les pneus.

The children are working.
Les enfants travaillent.

They write with pencils,
Ils écrivent avec des crayons,

paint pictures,
font de la peinture,

look at books
regardent des livres

and cut up paper.
et découpent du papier.

When the teacher is not looking,
Quand la maîtresse ne regarde pas,

Julie spills the paint,
Julie renverse la peinture,

squeezes the tube of glue,
presse le tube de colle,

climbs on the bookcase
monte sur la bibliothèque

and tears up paper.
et déchire du papier.

The workmen dig a hole in the ground.
Les ouvriers creusent un trou dans le sol.

- cement mixer — la bétonnière
- broom — le balai
- digger — la pelleteuse
- rail — la barre
- cement — le ciment
- motor — le moteur
- plank — la planche
- drill — le marteau-piqueur
- bricks — les briques
- trowel — la truelle
- shovel — la pelle
- tap — le robinet
- earth — la terre
- barrel — le tonneau
- hosepipe — le tuyau d'arrosage
- lamp — la lanterne
- boot — la botte
- pipe — le tuyau
- cat — le chat

They are putting in new pipes. One man
Ils posent de nouveaux tuyaux. Un homme

trips over a shovel,
trébuche sur une pelle,

falls in the cement,
tombe dans le ciment,

knocks over the drill
renverse le marteau-piqueur

and breaks a pipe.
et casse un tuyau.

We go to the hospital to see Granny.
Nous allons à l'hôpital voir grand-mère.

The nurses are very busy.
Les infirmières sont très occupées.

They make the beds,　　　　　　straighten the pillows
Elles font les lits,　　　　　　　redressent les oreillers

and give pills and medicine to the patients.
et donnent pilules et médicaments aux malades.

Sometimes we go to the swimming pool.
Parfois nous allons à la piscine.

- lifebelt — la bouée de sauvetage
- diving board — le plongeoir
- rail — la barre
- ladder — l'échelle
- swimsuit — le maillot de bain
- steps — les marches
- cap — le bonnet de bain
- lifeguard — le maître-nageur
- springboard — le tremplin
- mask — le masque
- goggles — les lunettes
- towel — la serviette
- float — la planche
- flipper — la palme

There are lots of people in the water.
Il y a beaucoup de monde dans l'eau.

A boy climbs the ladder and dives off the board.
Un garçon monte à l'échelle et plonge du plongeoir.

Julie wears a cap and swims with a float.
Julie porte un bonnet de bain et nage avec une planche.

It is windy.
Il y a du vent.

The kite flies away.
Le cerf-volant s'envole.

The leaves blow off the tree
Les feuilles s'envolent de l'arbre

and the little boat sails across the pond.
et le petit bateau navigue sur le bassin.

Uncle Paul gets out of the train,
Oncle Paul descend du train,

puts down his suitcase,
pose sa valise,

calls for a porter,
appelle un porteur,

trips over a mailbag
trébuche sur un sac postal

and hands in his ticket.
et donne son billet.

The train is ready to leave.
Le train est prêt à partir.

The signal goes green.
Le signal passe au vert.

The guard closes a door,
Le chef de train ferme une portière,

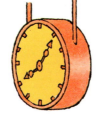

looks at the clock
regarde la pendule

and blows his whistle.
et siffle.

Here is a puzzle.
Voici une devinette.

Can you find the policeman, the motorcycle, a petrol pump, a bicycle and a taxi?
Peux-tu trouver l'agent de police, la motocyclette, une pompe à essence, une bicyclette et un taxi?

Pronunciation guide

There are some sounds in French which are different from any sounds in English. This pronunciation guide has been written to help you say the French words in the book correctly.

Below is a list of letters, with a guide to how to say each one in French. For each word, we have shown an English word, or part of a word, which sounds like it. Say these out loud to find out how to pronounce the French word, then practise saying the examples shown beneath.

a	like the "a" sound in *carrots*: ch<u>a</u>t, s<u>a</u>c
e	like the "e" in *the*: l<u>e</u>, d<u>e</u>
é	like the "ay" sound in *paper*: <u>é</u>vier, t<u>é</u>lévision
ê	like the "e" in *pencil*: b<u>ê</u>che, fen<u>ê</u>tre
i	like the "i" in *machine*: pol<u>i</u>ce, h<u>i</u>bou
o	like the "o" sound in *crayon*: c<u>o</u>ffre, br<u>o</u>sse
u	round your lips as if to say "oo", then try to say "ee": d<u>u</u>, <u>u</u>ne, b<u>u</u>lles
eau, au	sounds like the "oa" in *boat*: land<u>au</u>, mart<u>eau</u>, plat<u>eau</u>, f<u>au</u>teuil
eu	like the "or" in *worm*: d<u>eu</u>x, fl<u>eu</u>r
ou	like "oo" in *boot*: cl<u>ou</u>, r<u>ou</u>ge, p<u>ou</u>belle
oi	like the "wha" in *whack*: b<u>oî</u>te, <u>oi</u>seau
on, an	like "ong" without the "g": d<u>an</u>s, papill<u>on</u>
un	sounds like the "u" in *cup*, but do not say the n: <u>un</u>
in, ain, im	like "ang" in *hang* without the "g" at the end: tr<u>ain</u>, couss<u>in</u>
c	if before "i" or "e", it sounds like "s" in *sink*: <u>c</u>itron, <u>c</u>iseaux if before any other letter, it sounds like "c" in *carrot*: <u>c</u>oncombre, <u>c</u>apot
ç	like "s" in *saw*: gla<u>ç</u>age, balan<u>ç</u>oire
ch	is pronounced like "sh" in *shop*: bê<u>ch</u>e, <u>ch</u>ien
g	before "i" and "e", it sounds like the "s" in *measure*: rou<u>g</u>e, éta<u>g</u>ère before any other letter, it is like the "g" in *garden*: <u>g</u>âteau, ba<u>g</u>uette
gn	like the "ni" sound in *onion*: pei<u>gn</u>e, bai<u>gn</u>oire
j	like the soft "s" in *measure* above: <u>j</u>ardin, py<u>j</u>ama
th	sounds like "t" in *teddy*: biblio<u>th</u>èque
qu	like "k" in *kiss*: es<u>qu</u>imau, pa<u>qu</u>et
h	is not pronounced: <u>h</u>ôpital, <u>h</u>ache

A consonant at the end of a French word is not usually pronounced e.g. peti<u>t</u> (pe-tee), boi<u>s</u> (bwa), chie<u>n</u> (she-a), rideau<u>x</u> (rid-oh).